The Sufism of th

or, the Secret of the Great Paradox

Omar Khayyam

Alpha Editions

This edition published in 2024

ISBN : 9789364736794

Design and Setting By
Alpha Editions
www.alphaedis.com
Email - info@alphaedis.com

As per information held with us this book is in Public Domain.
This book is a reproduction of an important historical work. Alpha Editions uses the best technology to reproduce historical work in the same manner it was first published to preserve its original nature. Any marks or number seen are left intentionally to preserve its true form.

PREFACE

In placing this volume before the public I only hope that I may be able to convey to my readers the higher and deeper truths of this most famous of Persian Poets, who so ably attempted to portray to his countrymen the benevolent God the subtle life within the grosser of our material forms.

Also the mysterious force within the grape, which renders possible fermentation, thereby changing its character from matter to spirit. Therefore, I sincerely trust that this may be a means to enlighten many seekers after truth, and to my Critics will but add this line, "that they in me can find no opponent for them," for what little I have done has been to bless, to illuminate, not destroy the works of others, to whom myself with the rest of the world's readers owe our many thanks. Hoping that all may realize the spirit in which I here present it, and may it comfort and bless those who read to learn of its sublime truths, is the sincere wish of thy brother man.

THE AUTHOR.

NOTES

RUBÁIYÁT. A reading between the lines, a meaning within a meaning, a paradox.

OMÁR KHAYYÁM. The Tent Maker, an ancient Persian manner of expression signifying the Supreme Creator, for a tent to their minds represented the universe, the earth formed its level or floor, and the heavens its canopy. Again, the expression Astronomer Poet was another title for the Creator. He who laid out the heavens as a garden and placed the stars in design or order. He was also the Controller of the seasons, the Lord of the Vernal Equinox and the Prince of Horsemen.

IRAM. The nameless center of the universe, the womb from whence all things are born; the heavenly garden where Jamshyd the King of Splendor (or wisdom) sits enthroned, and reads from out the seven orbited cup (the inverted heaven) wherein the orbits of the seven planets circle around within its sphere, and there divines the astronomical mysteries of the seasons, years and all hidden things.

RUSTUM and ZÁL. The personification of the universal positive and negative creative energies, the elements of causation, the great opposites, summer and winter, youth and age, etc.

HÁTIM TAI. The personification of charity, benevolence and generosity.

TAKHT-I-JAMSHYD. The throne of wisdom, the mid-heaven, whereon Jamshyd the King of Splendor (or wisdom) symbolized by the sun when he reaches his zenith at high noon. The ancient Persians like the more modern Parsee do not worship the Sun as God, but to them it is the symbol of God, the All Seeing Eye, the Surveyor of the worlds, etc.

BAHRÁM GÙR. This character symbolizes the sun in the astronomical sign of Sagittarius wherein he represents the ass or old year, which will soon be lost in the swamps of winter or the sign of Capricorn, the extreme point of the southern ecliptic.

SATURN. Lord of the Seventh Heaven, the symbol of old age or ripeness.

MÁH to MÁHI. From fish to moon, an expression denoting the period from conception to birth, the state of transition between matter and spirit and between life and death, or as we use the same expression in the words "it is neither fish nor fowl."

PARWÌN. The Pleiades, the symbol of spirituality, gentleness, kindness, etc.

MUSHTARÌ. The Planet Jupiter, the symbol of benevolence, religion, toleration and big heartedness.

RAMAZÁN. The lunar month, beginning about the middle of March and ending about the middle of April; it is the Easter of the Mohammedans, the birth of regeneration or the spring.

The Sufism of the Rubáiyát

1

AWAKE! AWAKE! Oh, slumbering souls,

Arise like HIM who rules the morn and leads forth the stars with song.

Oh, Master hail to Thee! strike Thou with Wisdom's shafts the enemies of man's progression,

Thou who art known as the Dispeller of Mortal Darkness and the Light of the Life to Come.

Lead us by that Sure Path to where the SPIRITUAL SUN doth rise and where MORTAL DARKNESS sets beyond the clouds of FEAR, ANGER, SORROW, INDOLENCE and CRIME,

Where THE GREAT PEACE reigns and THOU OH LORD ABIDEST.

2

And before the [1]FALSE MORN of Earthly Life doth fade, that Voice Supreme within this TAVERN cries,

The Sacrifice is ready, loiter not outside, all is prepared, enter in, those wishing here to pray.

This is the way by which the soul doth learn, of GOD, of WORLDS, of THINGS KNOWN and UNKNOWN.

Whilst those who worship through man's carved creeds, pomps, rituals and dumb forms,

Worship like tongueless bells seeking to sound their tidings to the world.

All cries within THINK! THINK! THINK! It was not WORSE BEFORE, NOR BETTER THAN 'TIS NOW.

   [1] The False Dawn is the reflection of the coming day upon the horizon before the sun is high enough to reflect himself or the true dawn.

3

Then the Higher Nature springs up the old to greet, which always dwells within the doors where intelligence doth live.

And with a mighty shout calls OPEN WIDE! COME FORTH! MY PEACE I BRING, IN TRUTH I GREET ALL YE WHO LOVE THE TRUE.

Earthly Life is short; oh, slumber not I pray, for once ye have onward passed, prayers and repentance then are vain.

Seek while on earth the HEAVENLY GOAL to find, for MORTAL LIFE is short and comes but once!

Take heed, TIME IS LIFE'S JEWEL! MARK WELL, THIS IS THE WAY.

4

Thus the NEW YEAR OF LIFE has now commenced and the awakened soul is revived with a love of knowledge deep and true,

Which was written of by [2]MOSA, HE OF THE WHITENED HAND and TONGUE THAT WAS SLOW OF SPEECH.

Under the TREE of LIFE whose roots in the lives of all are planted deep.

This is the SAVIOUR OF WELL-BEING in which all EXISTENCE RESTS and BREATHES.

[2] The White Hand of Moses does not here signify leprosy, but the white hand of truth, honesty and friendship. It did not signify the color of his skin then, any more than it does now, but simply a moral qualification. Thus the white hand of Moses (or wisdom) was described by the ancient Hebrews as "One who was slow of speech;" and though apparently it may take longer to express itself than untruth or dishonesty in the realm of mental evolution, yet in the end its victory is complete.

5

The night indeed hath passed away, and with it gone that CAUSE OF ALL DECAY.

[3]The King of Splendor holding the Seven Orbed Cup of Wisdom to the earth,

Through which the Powers of Divination came to their birth in man; commanded, all life's powers to control, though living here in clay:

None but the Wise may DIVINE this POWER! Nor none may of its commencement know, nor of its end,

Till they the answer for themselves have wrung.

[4]Where gushes the RUBY of the VINE, that many a past recollection has stored in the Garden of Immortal Memory.

Which when watered by past experience brings forth WELL RIPENED FRUIT.

> [3] The King of Splendor here represents the transcending of the SUPREME INTELLIGENCE into the realm of intellect or the objective world.
>
> [4] Or the fountain head from whence flows the life forces.

6

[5]The soul of man, the LIPS OF THE BELOVED, in that high inspiring voice with which that INNER MAN doth speak,

Cries, LIVE! LIVE! Live an active useful life; the Nightingale, that Bird of night,

Calls to the Beauteous Rose that blooms by day, to bring life's color to her sallow cheek.

So doth this Voice Divine bid us, to turn to WINE the WATERS of DOUBT and COLD DESPAIR.

Thus the DEEP from out the DEEP doth call, in voice of thunder, HEAR ye all! MAN IS BORN TO LIVE.

> [5] The soul of man is here called the Lips of God, through which the Spiritual Voice speaks in a different tone, or a high, inspiring sound.

7

[6]Then take this CUP and with the FIRE of RESOLUTION fill, lay now aside forevermore those garments of FEAR and INDOLENCE.

The time on earth is far too short to waste on self upbraidings;

Nor stand ye shivering on the banks of repentance, but seek deliverance within.

For the BIRD of LIFE has TAKEN WING.

> [6] The cup here denotes the earthly life, which must be filled with resolution to succeed.

8

[7]Whether one in order or confusion lives, or whether one of the sweets of this life eats, which in the next the bitter must become,

[8]Or those who on the bitter live which in the next the sweet becomes; the LAW OF COMPENSATION surely straightens out.

The WINE of LIFE is KNOWLEDGE GAINED, on which no claims can Justice lay.

The LEAVES of LIFE are USELESS WORKS for which Justice decrees that RIGHTEOUS ONES MUST BE PERFORMED TO BALANCE LIFE'S ACCOUNT.

> [7] The sweets of this life refers to the worldly pleasure, the sensuous enjoyments, which retard our spiritual progress here and for which we suffer in the next if we become a slave to them in this life.
>
> [8] The bitter here refers to the virtuous, strenuous life, the life of denying, renouncing the so-called pleasures, the seeking to conquer our animal qualities.

9

Each month a thousand new thoughts bring but of the thoughts of yesterday which brought the [9]Summer Bearing Rose to view,

On which the King of Splendor sits and rules, all reverence be.

OH, THOU OF PRISTINE PURITY, MASTER AND DREAD JUDGE OF ALL THAT BREATHES, WHO ART THE LIGHT WITHIN THE LIGHT, AND WHO OF NO DISTINCTIONS KNOWS.

> [9] The Rose is here used as an interrogation point, meaning to ask the question, where springs forth the spirit of regeneration wherewith a man from evil is reclaimed?

10

Rest well content; what matters it to you, whether the dead do live? The quick do surely die.

Let argument and praise thunder as they may, and though the loud voice of orthodoxy bid you to the FEAST of DREAD, FEAR and ARROGANCE, take thou no heed.

All life and death are but transcending states, all is LIFE and all is DEATH to those who know where DEATH IS DEAD.

[10]Thus learn of sleep its opposite awake, from sorrow learn of joy, for between these PARALLELS doth that STREAM most surely flow,

Which is bereft of NAME, of FORM, of LIFE, of DEATH!

It is THAT which we know as THE INFINITE, from whence come all, and whither all again do go.

> [10] Death is not found in the state of Infinitude, thus death ceases to be when the Infinite is reached.

11

Thus between the lines of love and hate, of pure, and impure, the modest, and unchaste, lust of days and lust of fame,

The RIVER of CONTENTMENT smoothly flows.

The name of slave and monarch cease to be, PEACE IS THE NAMES OF ALL IN THE INFINITE UNITY.

12

The BOOK of LIFE beneath the [11]TREE, a [12]jug of wine, a loaf of bread, and thou, oh Memory, well stored with SACRED LORE,

What wilderness of life doth not then a paradise become?

> [11] The Tree of Knowledge.
>
> [12] The jug of wine here denotes the life of opportunities, the loaf of bread experience, with which we wisdom learn and thus memory perfect.

13

Sigh not in vain for what can never be, the glories of the morn depart as wanes the day.

So with each succeeding race to come the Christian Heaven or the Heathen Hell will but live in the dead words of memory.

Every generation a higher conception grasps of Creation's Laws the CAUSE DIVINE of LIFE.

So take the real, no matter what 'tis styled, whether GOD, JEHOVAH, CHRIST, or BUDDHA, DJAINA, BRAHM.

It is the same the sages say, though called by various names, and those who stand the PATH to bar,

Which unto that TEMPLE of SUPREME PEACE leads, are but the wanton enemies of GOD and MAN.

14

Look around and note what in all nature sighs of self:

Willingly she yields the bounty of her love, Spring unto Summer, Summer to Autumn pledged;

Winter that Chariot of Sorrow to the Steeds of Spring is yoked fast.

Live as it were in this sorrow, from its conquest comes the reward; what ended last night in tempest will with the dawn become calm.

That for which self in sorrow sighs, would surely if gratified sting, for real prayer cannot be offered, till the [13]HEART FROM DESIRE HAS BEEN FREED.

Hold thyself as the rose its petals, which when bloomed, casts its treasures of beauty and perfume, into the GARDEN called EARTH.

[13] Selfishness stands in the way of spiritual supplication; the prayers for the things which in themselves are forever changing cannot be profitable to any one, but the prayers which spring from the heart for its emancipation are the prayers which count.

15

Learn then in life from uselessness and use, and cast not aside OPPORTUNITY, YOUTH'S GOLDEN CROWN.

For they who shun such moments like desert wastes become, which must be dug and watered again and yet again,

Before the grain will start and bring forth well nourished fruit.

16

Vain are the worldly desires upon which men set their hearts: like a fool who in a mirror looks and wisdom there perceives,

So do the desires of men deceive them, for all CREATED THINGS do surely perish.

And though the like may prosper for awhile, there comes unerringly the fate to all structures that upon the sands are built!

They from sight for aye do pass away.

17

Think not this life of joy and woe the only life there is to know?

It is but here our earthly task, which when completed, fades from view, when its destined hour arrives,

INTO THAT PEACE WHICH FOR ETERNITY ENDURES.

18

[14]The Courts wherein the KING of SPLENDOR holds full sway, betwixt the EAGLE and the BULL and where the LION and the MAN do play;

HE there glories and drinks deep each day at noon, then falling from HIS throne is speeded to HIS doom.

This is the SPARKLING WINE of which all on earth may drink, that brings the harvest to the barn,

And is that GREAT CAUSE OF LIFE which none can turn, nor yet its harmony destroy.

[14] The Courts here represent the heavens, the King of Splendor the Sun in the month of JUNE when at twelve high noon the Sun is then in 15 degrees of Cancer, when the signs of TAURUS, Leo, Scorpio and Aquarius which form the signs of the Equinox are at the feet as it were of the Celestial King.

19

What puts value on some deed, some thought, some fondly cherished memory of a friend or future hope?

Answer you who value give and take, WORK! LOVE! GRIEF! and PAIN!

Work gives the value to deeds done and undone, love adds her charm as does the twilight to the sun;

Grief brings us fear, that subtle mental pain, which binds to earth, till DEATH THE KNOT UNTIES.

20

Ah, this [15]REVIVING HERB that's called the FUTURE STATE, upon its lovely lips, hangs the DEW OF HOLIER THINGS.

Thine is the [16]RUBY which is set in VIRGIN GOLD, and those who know the FOUNTAIN HEAD from whence streams forth that LIGHT DIVINE,

Have stood FACE TO FACE WITH GOD, and from the BONDS OF DEATH ARE FREE.

[15] The Reviving Herb stands here for immortality.

[16] The Ruby here represents the sum total of life's experience, which is set in Virgin Gold or the ring of eternity.

21

Thus break thou from this wheel of strife and stress, with all its sorrows, fleeting, joys and chilling fears;

Thine [17]arrow having plucked from out thy flesh, no more are pain and grief, thy sorrows ended are,

Tomorrow, what? [18]Thou with thy past totalities shall be joined again.

> [17] Pride, Anger, Fear, and Greed, which are the parents of all ills.
>
> [18] The unity with your past existences for life belongs to all times and to all planes.

22

That which is [19]FINITE is revealed, that which is INFINITE is concealed, this pair the part of Father and Mother play, till time their purpose doth make plain.

What to our senses seemed so fair, that which our minds so oft aside have cast;

That which in void and emptiness lay hidden, has the FAIREST of the FAIR become, when freed from PRISON.

> [19] The Finite is the objective or revealed, the Infinite is the subjective or concealed.

23

That which was the DARKNESS in the DARKNESS hidden, that which was joy enrobed in SORROW'S somber garb calls,

We who make merry in this hostelry of life, return the robe of earth to HIM who will another body make, for some soul to upward take, upon its homeward way.

24

The only thing of profit here to take is the Good from all things, which causes hurt to none.

Those who otherwise partake, the LAW pronounces invalid, which like the dust must to the dust descend.

Yet in that dust the GOLDEN GERM is found, which like a thought, a seed brought forth that ripened fruit may bear.

So comes forth again the BREATH, the BIRTH, the LIVING and the END.

25

Look not to the morrow to solve thy doubts, nor question oracles for good or better days,

As naught from the SILENCE SPEAKS but THOU, OH VOICE DIVINE, the DWELLER of the HEART, who biddest all perform good works.

No day on earth is better than the rest, each day is what you make it, neither more nor less.

They who deliverance seek beyond the clouds, and they who look for reward of good works done, both here themselves deceive.

REWARDS my friends are neither THEN nor THERE, REWARDS ARE SENT TO THOSE RIGHT HERE, WHO MAKE NO CLAIM ON MERIT WON.

26

Neither the sages of the past, nor those yet forth to come, nor what the books have said though of Holy Men inspired, do Him reveal.

To us HE only doth reveal HIMSELF in WORKS, in ACTS, in DEEDS done and undone, and by no other way may we hope HIM to KNOW or SEE.

It is but the foolish who cry I SAVE! I SAVE!! For unto the smallest insect, not again can they impart that BREATH DIVINE when it has onward fled.

Such claims as these, which some lips here do make, by WISER LORE are closed AT LAST.

27

Why then consult the Doctor or the Saint, they both from the same place came, and both to the same place go.

But if for confirmation of the Future Life ye seek, look to the Universe and know the same GREAT CAUSE that cast its mould gave you your birth of clay.

THINK! KNOW THAT THOU AND IT ARE PART AND PART, OF WHICH BEGINNING SAW NO DAWN, AND EVE NO ENDING.

The same doth regulate the hours, the days, the weeks, the years, the INFINITE TIME SPACE, and likewise thine.

28

This then is the Law of Fate and how of the way of Freedom all may learn, who freedom seek.

Know thou that THOUGHTS MATURE INTO DEEDS AND ACTS! AND ALL SEEDS SOWN IN THE FLESH SHALL RIPEN WITH THY YEARS.

This life is but the harvest of what you've sown before; sift out the tares before thou cast THE GRAIN FOR FUTURE YEARS.

29

Out of the Endless came I here! Into the Endless will I once more flow;

Out of it again in trust I come! Better for the TRAILS OF DUST BELOW.

30

Ushered into being by an Endless Unspent Cause which moveth unto good, and by all on earth adored.

Whence and where I went, only in deep reverence these words were spoke,

Oh Cup, from whence the very Gods have drunk, [20]EXPERIENCE is thy name, Oh let me freely drink from THEE, THOU SLAYER OF MY FOES.

[20] Experience is the only teacher, and thus becomes our liberator from the bonds of selfishness and greed, the parents of crime and ignorance.

31

What is it but madness to compare yesterday's sorrows with today's despairs, or tomorrow's triumphs?

For they but lend the means to quicken our perceptions of whence we came, why, and whither we go.

Drink thou of Life's Ruby Wine, and to those who dare for more to ask within themselves the answer will be found!

DRINK DEEP! THIS IS ENOUGH!!

32

[21]What if the Sun of the Moon should question WHY? What if the Stars of the World should ask, where did you die, for what, when and why?

Friends, deep in the hearts of all a Voice exclaims, cease, why, what, whence, and where, the solution thus, is never found.

Dismiss the I, dismiss the YOU, with you and I dismissed, the UNIVERSE is THOU, in which is found neither what, why, whence, where nor how.

[21] The moral to this paragraph is simply waste not your time in questioning, but act, and thus through action the knowledge you will gain.

33

Then waste not thy life in the letter of dispute, argument is death to the voicing of the Truth.

Religion debate with none. For it but tends to widen out the breach and thus defeat its ends.

Let thine acts declare the life within, happiness doth express the soul that dwells therein.

While SADNESS that BITTER FRUIT which has been here maintained, is the VINE from which all LIFE its being drew,

Ah friends, this is an error sad indeed, for HAPPINESS WAS THE GRAPE from which the WINE OF LIFE WAS PRESSED, NOT SORROW'S PRICKLY PEARS.

34

From those FAIR POINTS the [22]FIVE GREAT TRUTHS, by which we're raised by MASTER HANDS,

Their SECRETS then within the MAN are placed, GUARD WELL! For once REVEALED NO MORE CAN THEY BE HID!

Thus born of FIRE the CAUSE of LIFE SUPREME, in EARTH your soul was cast, in AIR thy thoughts took wing.

And from the BROODING WATERS, KNOWLEDGE took shape and came, as the means of man's DELIVERANCE from BIRTH and from the GRAVE.

This TRIPLE KNOWLEDGE has been told how EARTH the BODY is, and FIRE the SOUL, AIR is LIFE'S THOUGHTS, and the WATERS the SACRED LORE CONTAIN.

EARTH the INFANT, FIRE the YOUTH, the WATERS ENLIGHTENED MANHOOD, and AIR the CARRIER to the GREAT UNKNOWN BEYOND THE GRAVE.

Of which DEATH IS THE MESSENGER, NOT THE STING, and the GRAVE the SEPARATION OF LIFE'S ELEMENTS, AND HENCE THE VICTORY OF ALL LIVING THINGS.

[22] Here refers to our intellectual senses, or Intuition, Perception, Retention, Imagination and Analization, which raise us from our lower or physical conditions, and exalt us into our spiritual or higher nature.

35

Thus in the earth thy roots of life are struck, and from thy mother receive their nourishment.

Quickened into BEING by that CAUSE DIVINE, TO BE! WHO hands to thee the clay [23] to mould, Oh FRIEND, to mould?

[23] All beings are created equal, and each for himself must individualize his work or actions.

36

And this all here may know, how came the FIRST GREAT LIGHT to earth, that KINDLER of LOVE'S FLAME, that CONSUMER of earthly HATE.

When thou hast received one ray of this IMPERISHABLE LIGHT then thou art saved [24] THOUGH THY TEMPLE IS DESTROYED.

[24] When we can perceive that through our conventionalities and self formed opinions we delay our spiritual progress through limitations, we can then embrace the inclusive and forego the exclusive, thus changing our manner of living and entering the path that unto freedom leads.

37

Up to the Eternals cast thy weary eyes, earth is not thy home, no more than heavenly skies.

Question those Heavenly [25] Symbols of Mars the God of War, Jupiter of Benevolence, Mercury of Lore, Venus of Life's Pleasures.

Saturn of Old Age, ask Uranus of what is hidden, the Moon of Bringing Forth, and the Sun of Life's Fecundity, and each will in turn declare that they like thee are dependants,

Upon that ONE GREAT CAUSE to share, the knowledge of their being, which all may read WHO DARE.

[25] The planets, signs and constellations symbolized to the ancients the universal creative energies, their powers and equivalents.

38

Here then is the Key, thy Will that Door unlocks, thy Future Faith must be the KNOWLEDGE of THYSELF.

Shirk not this task for in it ye will find the way in which to solve, that the [26]UNIVERSE is I!

[26] Through the analyzing of our natures we learn that we are as it were a miniature of the universe and that we are potentially its equal.

39

Earth, Fire, Air, Water, Ether, the elements that compose the sum of all that under heaven blows,

And if ye then should ask, how they their birth received, or whence they came, or of what consist, or where they go, and of their final destiny?

THIS WILL ALL AGES ANSWER! HE ONLY KNOWS! HE ONLY KNOWS!

40

The Heavenly signs are but the SYMBOLS of that BOOK, whose chemistry Birth's secrets here make plain.

Thus are written in characters eternal, where none can erase one word of those recorded histories of MEN, of THINGS, of WORLDS.

From off its open pages bound in HEAVEN'S ETERNAL BLUE,

Here then is the VEIL, the LAMP, the VOICE WITHIN; learn thou to be LORD and MASTER, PROPHET, PRIEST and KING.

Thy BIRTHRIGHT here now enter, and know ye the LAW OF LAWS, the WISE MAN RULES, THE FOOL DOTH TREAD WHERE ANGELS FEAR TO GO.

41

Thus from the Law of Life and Death we learn, and why with hate and strife this earthly urn doth burn.

Yet a Voice from out of the DEPTHS doth SPEAK "MURMUR NOT"! Make ye the best of life,

Waste not thy OPPORTUNITIES! For when ye once have onward passed, to CLAY YE NEVER SHALL RETURN.!!

42

This is the way of Happiness and how to live free from vain regrets;

Whatsoever thy mind findeth to think, think ye only on such things as ye will never have to here unthink.

Whatsoever thy hands find to do, do only such things as ye will never have to here undo.

That which ye give, seek never to reclaim, nor profit make of friendship, nor from the STRANGER within thy gates, excepting what the LAW prescribes as lawful and as just,

This is an old but well proven Path, and KISSES FROM SUCH LIPS AS THESE DRY NEVER, NEITHER PARCH THEY THE MOUTH OF THE GIVER, OR THE GIVEN.

43

In passing through this Life of Clay, I came across a Barren Waste of life, and questioned of a friend its name, he answer made, INSANE! INSANƎ!

And when I asked if here the Potter's hand had not surely blundered, seeing so many monstrous shapes in clay called MAN,

He but answered "Nay, the same hand made the poison, that gave the antidote."

Ah, Friends and Foes, let us here unite, and make war on this all consuming vice; don't blame the Potter or his clay, we have but here OURSELVES to BLAME.

44

Listen a moment whilst I quote from a book that no man wrote; it is from Mother Earth, so friends give ear, attend! attend!

"It is you who knead and mould, not I, I'm but the plastic side of life, and THOU THE POTTER who doth spin this wheel of life continually."

Thus, Oh Brothers and Sisters learn, who will while here give birth to child,

Seek ye to mould it free from fear, seek ye to mould it strong and firm, let no thought its mind pervert, mould it TRUE and FIT for BIRTH.

MOULD IT FRIEND, OH MOTHER MOULD, IN THAT LIKENESS GOD OF OLD, THOUGH THY NAME ON EARTH IS MAN, YET OF THAT KINGDOM, PRINCE!.

A CHILD DIVINE ART THOU.

45

That which we mould again returns to earth, and this is a lesson, friends, which the Bright Ones unto thee have sent!

"The Beauteous Lily that neither toils nor spins will to the earth return again.

Pure was its perfume and its life, pure its color, snowy white; from its seed shall others come, which will bloom, then fade and die."

May we in such simple trust, hope again a lip to touch, FAIRER MOTHER, FAIRER CHILD, GOD and MAN UNITE AS ONE.

46

Let not this Cup of Life contain that Bitter Drug, Remorse by name, nor to Brother nor to Friend let us cause a burning tear;

Since these tears again give back SALT FOR SALT AND SMART FOR SMART.

Never let thy salt tears fall on this clay to bring forth more.

Drink not then from this Cup of Pain, for here is the secret of the Potter and his wheel—

Life is the clay with which the Soul doth spin, the Potter is the will by which the wheel is turned.

The Pot so called the Mind, which doth the thoughts contain, Experience is Life's Wheel which ACTION TURNS! Do Good, it recompenses with PEACE and BLISS, the EVILS here performed with PAIN and DEATH.

Thus do we learn of the unwinding of life's entangled skeins, of FEAR, of HATE and of all THINGS UNLOVABLE.

47

Yet there's another WINE which fresh from Life's vintage into the CUP OF IMMORTALITY is drawn.

[27]It is in color RUBY RED, resurrected from the DEAD. Drink ye! Drink ye! of this wine, the product of the VINE OF VINES.

They who from this CUP do DRINK with ETERNAL BLISS do meet.

Born of the perfumes of the flowers, watered by these tears of ours, nourished by the stress of life, OUR CROWN OF THORNS THE CROWN OF GLORY WINS.

> [27] The grapes must pass through the press to give up the wine; so must we through our earthly experience give up the material before we can accept the spiritual.

48

So when Death's Angel doth us call, instead of pains its joys we know.

The FEARS AND STINGS OF DEATH WERE MADE BY EARTHLY PRIESTS BUT NOT THE POTTER'S GENTLE HANDS.

This dark wine quaff and the cup to earth return, for you that stream have crossed and the further shore attained.

There's where thy soul its heavenly garb assumes, of which this dust of earth is too gross its frame to build.

49

This life is but the Pathway that unto FREEDOM LEADS, from pains and greivous sorrows, to where the soul is free.

To roam to worlds and spheres sublime and gather there from off the vines those ripened grapes for wine.

From limits then it's freed and towards its sun it soars, and there in BLISS SUPREME THAT SOUL IN GOD IS MERGED.

50

Thus the body is a tent wherein the soul a day or so must dwell, when Death again that life relieves,

And that freed soul above must speed to some new realm of thought unknown to it.

Would that all this simple truth did know, there would be then no fear of that after life to come.

51

Here then we learn that Law of Fate, as into this world we're born from different planes of life.

And here we all must tarry till this Earthly Life has run, when turning down this earthen cup,

The fluid of the soul is poured into a vase of finer ware.

Countless thousands have come and gone through these SILENT GATES OF FATE,

Which but open once for birth, then close till death, as ripples follow ripples on a wind swept lake.

52

Thus do we lift veil after veil before, thus do we drop veil after veil behind,

Onward, ever onward, do all who are born progress, none from this wheel break free, none can this law control.

Born of endless rounds, from sphere to sphere we climb, through countless suns of systems, through countless terms of years.

Systems of worlds we leave, whilst approaching unknown suns, with colors of nameless hues, for which no tongue a name hath found.

ON THOSE HEAVENS THE SUNSETS REST, AND THE TINTS OF THE MORNING SKIES.

53

Ah, questioning Friend, what is it you would know, from whence Existence came, and how Existence stays?

This is the Cross you'll carry, as long as you will cast the RUBY of the PRESENT in the DUST HEAP OF THE PAST.

It was not BORN, nor does it ever DIE; it from no place came, nor of anything was it; UNBORN, ETERNAL, EVERLASTING, DEATHLESS, IT WILL REMAIN, though all should PASS AWAY.

This is the Secret that the Wise alone can solve, how EXISTENCE the thread doth cut, which perchance divides those FOUR.

THE FINITE FROM THE INFINITE, AND THE FALSE FROM EVERY TRUE.

54

Could you right here this problem solve of what is false and true, no more would heaven yonder be, no more would erring thought heaven's truths obscure,

For at last the false is here out grown, and the Finite Mind ceases to reflect the evils of the past, which are forever lost in forgetfulness;

And only the Infinite Thoughts (which are life's pearls) are then reflected in that Mind Supreme.

So whilst in this home of clay we live, could we for a moment grasp this CAUSE SUPREME in its entirety, which moveth all, that life doth know, to GOOD, TO BETTER, THEN TO BEST;

God will here and there alike be known, and of that SUPREME PEACE we will stand on earth possessed.

So seek within this TREASURE HOUSE, for the KEY you'll surely find, which will unlock the Palace Gates and all mysteries there contained.

And seated there, all pure and white, that KING OF KINGS who reigns supreme is known of all celestial hosts, as THOU, OH SOUL, DIVINE.

55

A secret here I have to tell which I'll write between these lines, how one may find [28]the SERPENT COILED within the HUMAN SPINE.

Deep in the Breath of the Senses its secret presence you will find, running divided, yet united, it is the BREATH OF LIFE DIVINE.

It brings to name and form all thought, and though these change and pass from sight, it ever here remains to bring that WISDOM OF THE GODS TO MEN.

[28] This means the seat of all functional activity.

56

Look to thy body there to find the Mystic Numbers it contains, the Coccyx Four on which the Sacrum Five do rest, where spirit matter joins, and the TREE OF LIFE AGAIN PUTS FORTH.

Upon this NINE, though to FIVE this NINE returns, rest the DORSAL TWELVE, the Sacred Temples of those Mysteries from which the tribes of IS and RA were named,

In the Cervical Seven dwell supreme THOSE POWERS OF GOD ENTHRONED IN MAN; these do contain the THREE IN ONE of which the ages have all sung, about that TRINITY SUBLIME which moves the worlds to GOOD.

Now THREE in ONE, and FOUR PLUS FIVE, and TWELVE plus SEVEN, and you have found those MARKS THIRTY AND TWO OF PERFECT BIRTH.

57

There is a LINE that all may find, stretched from the utmost heavens (or maybe far beyond) which towards the earth comes unerringly,

Which has by all Sages here been called "THE PLUMB LINE OF THE UNIVERSE," adored and reverenced by all the Wise.

And where this Line the Earth doth GREET the LEVEL FORMS on which all MEET,

There the SETTING SUN YOU WILL THEN FACE, AND LIFE'S FATAL SQUARE will upon THEE FALL NO MORE.

Being thus FREE and ACCEPTED of the GODS, RAISED by the MASTER'S HANDS, EXALTED from the DEAD, to GREET again, and yet again, THY BRETHREN.

Brothers, tell them who have the rule forgot, how time is measured dot by dot; how the MASTER from the EAST must RISE and in splendor sit upon the noonday skies.

How at HIGH TWELVE upon that ARCH DIVINE HE SITS, and the QUARTERS of the world doth there survey each noon.

And upon that [29]TRESTLE-BOARD, which is watched and guarded by the FOUR REGENTS, HE the orders writes, for the MASTERS to transcribe.

Then that MYSTIC LINE HE crosses and hastens to HIS FALL, and thus are the days all reached, in which HE and all HIS FELLOW-CRAFT REPOSE MUST SEEK.

None can here deny that this forms not a perfect day, for it has been TRIED and PROVED by that UNERRING LINE.

NO YESTERDAY, NO TOMORROW, ALL IS ENDLESS DAY ENWRAPPED IN ENDLESS NIGHT, IN WHICH ALL SLEEP, IN WHICH ALL WAKE, BOTH HERE AND THERE.

[29] These Jewels of Masonic Lore must appeal to all true readers of the TRESTLE-BOARD. May they hear the fraternal voice of the past, which is now speaking through the lips of the present, and seek that reward which alone can come when the earthly lodge is closed and the heavenly is declared open for the work to all who have been found worthy and qualified.

58

Thus in the hands of mortals are placed the BUILDER'S TOOLS, the PLUMB, the GUIDING LINE 'twixt HEAVEN and the TOMB.

The SQUARE most blessed of all KNOWN TOOLS for it reveals THAT GLORIOUS CROSS from which the WISE their LORE OF LIFE HAVE GAINED.

And though it's hidden FOURFOLD DEEP its ROOT can be obtained, which will the CUBE-STONE form again, OH, MYSTERY SUBLIME.

Born thus of Earth, by Air, by Fire and Water Tried, NAILED to the CROSS the PROOF OF LIFE TO FIND.

Ushered in the EAST the way of birth for all, in the SOUTH is MANHOOD reached, in the WEST where all must FALL, it is the PLACE OF PEACE which all must haste to reach;

It is there that you MARK WELL and the FATAL SQUARE REVERSE, the NORTH of DEATH doth know from whence ye have come forth,

To take within thy hand THE BUILDER'S MYSTIC TROWEL.

59

And having built my EARTHLY HOME, one day in its porch I sat, and coming through its shades and glooms was a FACE THAT FIXED ITSELF upon my memory.

It was my SOUL INVISIBLE that brought a MESSAGE DIVINE, which from EARTHLY FETTERS SAVED ME and in FREEDOM bade me RISE;

To those EFFULGENT SKIES OF SKIES, the FOUNTAIN HEADS FROM WHENCE DO FLOW THE WATERS OF ETERNITY.

And from a CHALICE wrought of GOLD the WINE of IMMORTALITY WAS POURED and having drunk that Wine of Wines, I returned the [30]Cup which from Gold was made.

[30] The Cup wrought out of gold here refers to our collective experiences.

60

Thus having quenched my thirst of years wherefore I asked of Him, are there so many here, who spend their lives in tears,

And waste their days in arguments over what is RIGHT or WRONG?

He in these powerful words His answer gave!

"ALL MEN AND WOMEN WERE EQUAL MADE! AND OF TEARS AND SORROWS GAVE HE NONE TO MAN; NONE CAN SUFFER EXCEPT THOSE WHO SUFFERING CHOOSE."

Which sufferings being but DELIVERANT PAINS OF BIRTH, GIVE TO THE SOUL ITS FREEDOM.

To my second question He answered thus!

WHO DARES OF RIGHT OR WRONG TO JUDGE, since the motive of a crime in ages past has disappeared, and crimes that were unknown to them are living here with you?

But to those who seek TRUE JUDGMENT this is the way it's found!

There is a Judge who never errs who sits in the human heart, whose judgments are not heard without, but in life's deeds are PROVEN.

No human tongue can yet define, nor will it here be given, that power on earth to understand the INFINITE LAW OF HEAVEN.

61

To meet my needs through life he gave these beauteous words of praise!

THOU MIGHTY PEACE, TRUTH BREATHING LORD, OF ALL THE HORDES OF DARKNESS AND OF LIGHT ADORED.

THOU subduer of fears and sorrows which this earthly life infest, and LEADER FORTH TO THAT FUTURE REST BEYOND THE GRAVE, WHERE DWELL THE SAGES OF ALL THE PAST.

In that NAME thy refuge seek, take thou thy refuge in its LAW OF PEACE, take thou its hand of FUTURE HOPE, and rest thou in its LAW which worketh unto GOOD, to BETTER and to BEST.

Thus was I taught of the LOVE DIVINE.

62

[31]This life is the vine on which the grape doth grow, and fresh from its PRESS THE WINE OF LIFE DOTH FLOW.

And there on the WASTE HEAP of sorrow lies the PULP OF WANTONNESS, from which the fool a strong and hurtful beverage brews, that works DESTRUCTION UNTO ALL WHO OF IT DRINK!

THEY WHO ARE CLEAN NEED NO STIMULANTS, EXCEPT THAT ONE CONTAINED WITHIN THE VINTAGE OF LIFE'S EXPERIENCE.

All other wines are rods of pain in which REMORSE IS FOUND in many garments dressed. BEWARE! BEWARE!!

Many men do question thus, Why was it put here if a curse? The swine the question here might put, Why must he eat what's on him thrust?

Present no more such reasoning pray for the answer is here given.

NONE BUT THE FOOL THE WINE OF EARTH DOTH QUAFF, NONE BUT THE WISE THE WINE OF LIFE DO DRAW.

[31] All that this life is, is the sum total of what the preceding one was.

63

Here I am compelled to write about another form of vice; some endure it in its LEGAL FORM whilst others are slaves to a NAMELESS FORM;

Never Brother, never Friend, wreck thy life on the shoals of shame, nor cast thy virtue in the dust.

NO TWO WRONGS WILL ONE RIGHT MAKE, NO HANDS IN PRAYER CAN A FOUL DEED CHANGE, OR A VIRTUE MAKE!

Ah, this is the BITTER CUP OF LIFE and whosoever from it drinks, into the dust descends. BEWARE! BEWARE!!

64

The means that do the ends of life defeat, are: DRINK! FORNICATION and other UNLAWFUL ACTS committed by the FLESH, GAMBLING and UNTRUTH.

No threats of HELL, no hope of HEAVEN, can lift the cloud that doth enshroud a DEFILED EARTHLY TEMPLE.

SUCH FLOWERS AS THESE FOREVER DIE, USELESSNESS HAS NO PLACE IN CREATION'S FERTILE FIELDS.

65

Oft has the WAY on earth been blazed, that all the PATH might see and rightly follow.

Sages the [32]PATERAN have placed at every crossroad.

And though so many have pushed those DARKENED DOORS aside, NONE HAVE RETURNED OF THAT WAY HERE TO TELL!

WHICH TO DISCOVER, ALL FOR THEMSELVES MUST TREAD.

> [32] Pateran means a leaf which travelers used to place at the cross roads to show the way to their followers.

66

Yet some may question the Wisdom of the Law, that FREE SALVATION grants to ALL ON EARTH WHO FALL.

Yet falling they must rise again, OH SLAYER OF OUR FOES, RENUNCIATION IS THY NAME!

With THEE we fight the hordes of PAIN, and PASSION SLAY, and thus destroy the CAUSE OF ALL OUR ILLS.

EACH HIS OWN SALVATION WINS! EACH ALL EARTHLY SIN MUST HERE RENOUNCE! THUS HAVE THE WISE ALL TAUGHT.

67

Let us call HIM THE ALL MERCIFUL for HE the PATH doth LIGHT, so man from MORTAL DARKNESS may be led into the LIGHT.

Hear ye then this simple, yet most ancient of the truths, how man can gain the knowledge of life beyond the tomb.

"CONTROL THYSELF, and with thy senses send thy soul unto its elements, there to wring out the SECRET of its BIRTH and END."

And the gentle voice of the SILENCE whispers soft and low, and bids me reader, write you the answer here below!

I MYSELF AM HEAVEN, I MYSELF AM HELL, I AM THE CAUSE CREATIVE, I AM THE WAY, THE END.

68

This then is a vision of heaven that FULFILLER OF ALL DESIRES, and this is the shade of GEHENNA the sorrows that life acquires.

Cast thyself boldly on this ocean, FEAR NOT THOUGH THE CURRENT IS STRONG, thy body's the BOAT, thy WILL the HELM, thy LIFE the SAILS doth fill.

And serenely sitting, all composed, thy Soul doth grasp the helm and steers thy Barque through storms and stress, in safety past the SHOALS of DEATH.

With its cargo that's consigned to HIM WHO RULES THE WINDS, THE TIDES, OH MASTER PILOT, HAIL TO THEE! THOU GIVER OF ETERNITY.

69

Coming events their shadows cast, on this all have agreed;

In an endless procession that Mirror reflects the acts, the thoughts, the deeds,

Oh, happy the man who has led a good life, who fears not in that Mirror to gaze,

For he sees that VIRTUE REWARD HATH WON, AND THAT THE WAGE OF SIN IS DEATH.

70

Some in this life would have you believe that this FATE you cannot evade, for all EMBODY here again, and thus by the LAW OF BIRTH outrun the ACTIONS of PAST LIVES?

Friends, you're reasoning in quicksands which in the end engulf; last night no more returns to earth though followed by countless suns;

Neither the soul once freed from clay to a body of clay returns, nor doth the Spirit inhabit again this cast off garment of earth.

THIS IS THE LAW; OH MORTALS LEARN, ALL YE WHO LOVE THE TRUE.

71

This is the LAW of LIFE written bold that all may read aright and learn THE WAY OF MASTERSHIP!

THOUGHTS ARE THE SHUTTLE OF LIFE'S WORKS, EXPERIENCE THE WARP, AND LIFE THE WOOF,

THE CLOTH THE DEEDS WHEN SPUN, which cut according to RIGHT MEASUREMENT fit well, and the garment of every soul becomes.

REASON MEASURES ALL! AND WISDOM GUIDES, and thus are the garments of life both small and great by a strict measurement made, wherein the law declares.

THOU THYSELF THE LAW OF LIFE DOTH RULE; LIFE! THOU ART RULED BY ALL THE WISE;

HE WHO THUS DOTH KNOW, KNOWS ALL IN LIFE TO BE, AS THE FUTURE LIFE'S DETERMINED BY THE PRESENT ONE WE LEAD.

72

[33]There is a GARDEN of which the Wise have told, with a RIVER that flows throughout, which when divided has FOUR HEADS, Oh, Students find this out.

There is a "WORD" the Wise declare though "LOST" it's yours to find, that would unite these FOUR again; of this there is no doubt.

It is FOUR-FOLD when opened out and the CROSS it brings to view; your life's engraved upon its "SQUARE" of which no erasion can be made nor "THY MARK" carved there be effaced.

[33] This paragraph refers to the center of creative energy or the Garden of Iram. The Four Rivers symbolize the seasons, body, mind, soul, spirit, earth, fire, air, water, in their process of ivolution and evolution and its symbolic character is the Swastika Cross.

73

This inverted bowl we call the sky, is that Garden we've been told; the FOUR HEADS there have thus been named the LION, the MAN, the BULL, the BIRD.

[34]Within these names four more are found; SPIRIT, SOUL, MIND, and BODY and yet again four more you have BIRTH, YOUTH, MANHOOD and AGE.

When added TWELVE all told they make, and the names of the TRIBES reveal, from which all things their being take, and yet there are four to spare;

REPTILES, BEASTS and BIRDS of song, with FISH of various kinds, when added go to make the MAN, OF SIXTEEN PARTS ALL TOLD.

[34] This paragraph gives the symbolic names of the divine qualities that are found in man.

74

Who then doth hold this SECRET of the WAY, which from this CARNAL HOUSE of clay to FREEDOM makes?

Or are we like the ever changing sea, IMPOTENT to change its currents or the wind?

It is only a sluggard who doth question the reason of his birth; the Brave like soaring eagles rise high above the earth,

They but know the PATH of DUTY, its GOLDEN WAY they tread, where trod the ANCIENT FATHERS who dissolved this life of earth.

Thus look not on HIGH the GOOD TO FIND, nor search for it BELOW; GOOD IS THE WHOLE, AND DEATH BUT LIFTS THE SCENES AS THEY UNFOLD.

75

This world no more endures than THOU or I, only the MAKER for 'twas HE who loosed its soul and thine to learn,

From whence came all, to where all go, the destiny, the end.

And should'st thou not learn from whence all pain doth spring, as ripple follow ripple so doth pain forever follow pain.

Till FREED FROM SENSUOUS YEARNINGS, THY HEART TO GOD RETURNS,
THIS IS THE FINAL CONQUEST, THIS IS THE FINAL END.

76

And thus was man made and placed in this GARDEN OF IRAM fair, with his soul to comfort and give cheer, till DEATH makes free again.

He in this INVERTED BOWL is poured, and there must remain 'tis said, till dust to dust returns again and that FREED SOUL has winged its way to where the DEATHLESS DWELL.

77

He out of his earthly origin wrought his desire for upward striving, for the Wise the RIGHT do prefer to the SWEET,

Whilst the Foolish the SWEET do prefer to the RIGHT and thus they're bound on this WHEEL of PAIN till they the KNOT untie again,

Which is the END AND THE BEGINNING OF THINGS.

78

Now in this GARDEN a SERPENT was placed and a man from the hand of a woman did taste,

Not the WOMAN of this CLAY nor any FRUIT of earthly NAME, but EXPERIENCE wrung from life and handed down from birth to birth.

GOD HAS JOINED THESE TWO IN ONE, WEDDED HERE FOR LIFE TO COME, EVER FAITHFUL! EVER GOOD! THEY MAY HERE BE UNDERSTOOD.

79

[35]He ate of the GOOD and the EVIL OF FRUITS from the hand of the woman who dwelt by his side,

And after he'd tasted he stood face to face with the laws he had taken in vain.

The bitter thus changed the sweet did become, hate changed to love and sorrow to joy, strife had ceased and peace had come.

When he had thus conquered lust, he had also conquered thirst; that man from pain doth free become, WHO THE BATTLE WINS, THAT CONQUERS SELF.

[35] One must always taste of his thoughts, deeds or actions and whether they are sweet or sour that alone depends upon our actions; and likewise our past lives must forever stand beside us, like a loving wife sharing our joys or sorrows and comforting in the time of need.

80

And if but for the asking all wisdom could be thine, what value would'st thou place upon things thus obtained?

Work makes the value, values cares do bring, cares bring forth sorrow, Death's complaisant friend.

Few from this womb are born that to maturity arrive; it is here that all values end and it is here that they all begin.

81

And under cover of departing day, slunk hunger stricken Doubt away, and with its departure came back once more the light of reason and passed within my door.

Again strange shapes I did behold in clay, and one came forth and licked my hand; it was a DOG!

And of the Potter I did ask, why sunk so low at birth was such a faithful soul?

The Potter merely turned his wheel and there upon the further side of a beauteous vase I beheld a wondrous design, executed with great skill.

It was a Temple to the Great and holding one of its main supports was a DOG! And at its base was carved these words in bold relief:

"PILLAR OF FAITHFULNESS TO MAN I GAVE; DOG WAS THY NAME ON EARTH, BUT FAITHFULNESS IN HEAVEN."

82

Some of the shapes were large, some small, and some were rough and some were smooth, and as the Potter turned the last, I saw it was a MAN.

Out of the earth had he been wrought, by experience he was taught; out of the VOICELESS came he here, into the VOICELESS will he once more pass.

OH, THOU WONDROUS VESSEL, THOU! LEARN TO KNOW THAT GOD IS MAN.

83

Shaped as a man again a vase I saw; it looked so smooth, so bright and tinted with colors rare,

All looked harmonious without, a beauteous vessel one would say, but to the Potter's knowing eye it was a FRAUD!!

And taking a mallet in his hand he beat it back to dust again.

And when I questioned why he had thus done, he paused and answered "It's not true."

This was the life of one on earth who never had his second birth; all things wished for had he there BOUND TO GREED! A SLAVE TO FEAR!!

Then the Potter a vase of modest form did show, but oh, how exquisite was it in comparison with the former ware.

The Potter answered "THE SAME SOUL DWELLS HERE NOW IN PEACE SUPREME."

THUS PASSED TO GREATER THINGS THAT SOUL OF YORE.

84

Then a beautiful vase of a maid I saw and by it standing in the gloom and shade was another of a man!

Both were covered deep in dust; it was a LESSON THUNDERED BACK TO EARTH, how both of them from LUST HAD DIED and destroyed the purpose of their lives.

And on a column reaching high these words burst forth in fiercest flame:

"THE CURSE OF LIFE IS LUST OF SEX AND THE COMMITTING OF ACTS UNLAWFUL AND UNFIT."

85

And in the corner of the Potter's shed stood a mighty vase, in shape a BULL, and this was written o'er his head:

PILLAR OF ENDURANCE cast in clay, thy name on earth is BULL; as a SIGN in the heaven I placed thee there that all on earth might read

That when thou bathed in the Sun's bright rays the Spring Time would begin,

So let men their trials with endurance meet and begin their Spring Time here,

And let the Fruits of Life mature and be RIPENED FULL BY FALL.

86

And some were crusted with old age, and some were bright as from the Potter's hand they came,

But neither YOUTH nor AGE could tell who was the POT, the POTTER or the MOULD,

They only knew that ONE GREAT CAUSE CREATED ALL! And then again dissolved.

HE MADE THEM ALL! TO HIM AGAIN THEY WENT! THIS WAS HIS SECRET; search it out they said,

Then of the difference ye will know between the POTTER, POT and THEE.

87

More strange, more fair, more beautiful designs I saw of leaves, of blooms, of ferns, of flowers, the choicest of the choice.

And such wild flowers, the like I had never seen before, which from the tropics and temperate zones of earth had come.

And others of color wondrous fair from the depths of the ocean were also there,

To compare with the flowers of earth the richness of their marine birth

All had been spun on the self same WHEEL, all to the earth their lives will yield,

Except their beauty and perfume, which with their SOULS TO HIM HAVE GONE.

88

All is thus spun by the POTTER on his WHEEL, in his shop the UNIVERSE, wherein he GRINDS, then KNEADS, then FIRES the LIVES of ALL, into shapes and things most lovable.

NAUGHT DOTH HE WASTE IN ALL HIS WORKS, FOR WHAT HE MAKETH UNTO TODAY HE MAKETH UNTO ETERNITY.

89

Thus do all things speak of HIM in praise, LORD OF HEAVEN, CREATOR and the GRAVE,

[36]OF WHOM PRIESTS AND WARRIORS BUT HIS DIET FORM WITH DEATH FOR SEASONING.

Thus the earth her welcome sings to the WATER CARRIER SPRING, who with his RAIN SKIN on his back calls to the WINTER, BACK! BACK! BACK!

Then he gently pulls the strings, COMFORTER DIVINE IS HE, sending down those warming rains on the barren thirsty plains.

THIS THEN IS THE HOLY SPIRIT WHICH FROM HEAVEN UNTO MAN IS GIVEN.

> [36] This means that He is both the Container and the Contained, that before Him there can be no Priest or Warrior, for He is the Divine of all forms of Rituals and Authority.

90

The VINE NEW LEAVES DOTH NOW PUT FORTH and the GRAPES though sour at first SWEETEN WITH THE SUN.

So may we bring this life of ours to close, for the GRAPES OF YOUTH will ripen with the FROSTS of YEARS.

Then shrouded in the LEAVES WHICH FROM THE TREE OF LIFE HAVE BROKEN FORTH IN THIS VINEYARD OF OUR LIVES WE ARE LAID AWAY TO REST.

There facing the RISING SUN, THAT RESPLENDENT MESSENGER OF HIM WHO IS FOREVER NAMELESS,

WE'LL BRING TO AGE AGAIN A BETTER GRAPE FOR WINE.

91

Here is where our dust is mingled with the earth that goes to nourish all unborn vines;

Think then of thy DEEDS, thine ACTS and THOUGHTS in LIFE, for they the nutrition form, with which the future vines are fed.

Would that all dust could return to earth as pure as when it first gave man this GARMENT FOR HIS SOUL.

92

HE who fashioned all so fair, HE who gave that GREAT COMMAND, HE whose LOVE IS INFINITE, HE whose BREATH IS PEACE DIVINE,

Wilt thou Doubter here declare WHO PERISHES, WHEN and WHERE?

Each for himself this NOBLE PATH doth tread, each for himself the CROWN of LIFE must WIN.

Unto thee, oh, DOUBTER hear! What HE CREATED IN HIS LOVE SHALL NOT BY WRATH BE HERE OR THERE DESTROYED!

93

Let all men dwell in PEACE and FREEDOM and bring forth those beauteous flowers that they have learned to cultivate.

Then thine will be a kingdom of blooms most rare, wherein the WEEDS OF REMORSE AND SHAME CAN NO HIDING FIND.

All will work towards that END DIVINE, to ILLUMINATE NOT DESTROY THE SPIRITUAL GARDENS OF THE MIND.

Then will the VINES of LOVE, TRUTH, PEACE and CHARITY flourish, and all will be in HARMONY WITH GOD; THIS IS OF THINGS THE END!

94

In a Garden where such Vines do climb there can be found no INFIDEL!!

AH, INFIDEL, THOU ART THE FRUIT OF PRIESTLY ARROGANCE.

May peace be granted unto them who sought thy mind to here enslave.

BEFORE HIM THERE IS NO PRIEST, INFIDEL, PAGAN, NOR HEATHEN; ALL ARE CALLED FRIENDS.

NO MORE MAY THESE HARD NAMES BE SPOKEN; THEY ARE UNLAWFUL AND UNFIT AND THEY THE LOVE OF GOD DENY WHO UTTER THEM.

95

When these names no more are heard, the ROSE OF LOVE puts forth, and perpetual youth doth greet the sons of every clime.

Upon the branches of the trees perch the [37]Eagle and the Dove, and the [38]Tiger with the Lamb at the River side make play.

This is a view of heaven that unto man descends; THE NIGHT INDEED HAS PASSED, THE DAY HAS DAWNED.

> [37] The Eagle and the Dove here describes the forces of sympathy and antipathy which form a duality within our natures, which when conquered by love cease to be active, hence we become at peace with all.

[38] The Tiger and the Lamb typify the physical and spiritual of our natures which so long as they are not absolutely controlled are at variance with ourselves, till love vanquishes greed, selfishness and avarice; then we learn that matter and spirit harmonize when properly adjusted.

96

Every desert will then have its spring, and every man and woman will have found that FREEDOM IS THE GOAL FOR LIFE TO WIN.

Making the best of what doth here befall, and to live in that PEACE which COMFORT BRINGS TO ALL.

97

Ah, thou Angel, of Repose! Fan thou the brow of those who suffer PAIN and in their EAR THAT MAGIC WORD IMPART,

That turns the fear of DEATH INTO LIVING THOUGHTS OF LOVE.

Bid all AWAKE and RISE and for evermore lay their ACHES and PAINS ASIDE,

To this end were they born, NOT SLAVES, FEARING TO LIVE, NOR LIVING, FEAR TO DIE.

98

And now my pen in honor here doth write, in praise of THEE thou SOUL DIVINE OF LOVE.

THOU ART THE CONQUERER OF THIS SORROW PILE OF LIFE, THOU ART THE SONG, THE SINGER AND THE DANCE.

Thou art the shade of all repose and peace; better thy smile than a TRIUMPHANT WREATH.

Better thy FRIENDSHIP THAN A MONARCH'S WEALTH, STRONGER THY HAND THAN ALL ARMED FORCE.

Fountain Divine, thou LIFE OF ALL that's born, THOU RUBY OF THE WINE, thou PERFUME OF THE MORN.

Friend and light of the wintry path, the dew drop's sparkle, and the flame that burns.

Comforter divine, thou art the wine that cheers; may we ever of thy vintage drink.

99

Once more the Moon has waned and fulled, and with each wane and full many have come and many passed away.

Still many more shall come, and many more will follow when she again in glory robes herself.

Silently she comes, silently she departs; she brings to age the life of every mortal.

And as the Night the Day removeth, so doth she the human generations.

100

Ah, Earthly Home, my last clasp now I take, of all thy pleasures and thy sorrows a fond farewell.

Oh, piteous and most fair! I've loved thee as a lover, and for my misdeeds let none other suffer.

Forgive the sins that I've committed; what I to others have done, may they in mercy pardon.

And as succeeding generations follow may they but know thee as thou art.

Farewell! Farewell! Oh, Father! Mother! Teacher! May this my dust be mingled once again with thine,

And o'er my tomb let the Flurring Petals of Autumn Blooms keep the Vigil of this my last of many sleeps.

The Murmuring Winds shall chant the mizzeran for the soul that's dead to earth,

And in thy gentle arms, Oh, mother, yield I up this life forever! Farewell!! Farewell!!!